POP,
you because you
...w to play marbles and you
...s with me. I Love You!!

Love you
Jamie
age 9

Dear Grandma,
I love you so much because
how much you love me, because
the way you hug me tight, because
how you love me too.

Love, Your
Grand child
Cassie

Age 8½

Dear Kathie
From one Grandma-to-Be
to another
With love
Dalia

8/21/05

Dear Granpa,
I love you because
you always let me Drive
the tractors and you...
have my favorite meal...
let me pick the me...
and play with the cat...

Love,

Dear, Grandma,
I love you because you give me
things and treat me good. You are
the best.

Love,
Austin
age 8

Dear Grandad,

I love you because you taught
me how to go fishing and use tools.
Thank you for teaching me how.

Your Granddaughter,

Vicki
age: 9

Dear, gramom

I Love you because you are gratist and best gramom
I ever had. xoxoxoxoxoxo when ever I come over you are
allways their for me. when I need you!!! I don 4
no what I would out you!!!!!!!

I Love You gramom
I Love Kevin

The GiFTs of being Grand

is dedicated to Grandma Mary, Nana Richmond,
Grandpa Jerry and Papa Richmond ... for being so grand! —MR

A special thank you to Ms. Megan Scully's 3rd grade class at
Bobby's Run School in Lumberton, New Jersey. Their notes
to their grandparents are a treasured part of this book.

Marianne Richmond Studios, Inc.
420 N. 5th Street, Suite 840
Minneapolis, MN 55401
www.mariannerichmond.com

ISBN 1-58209-839-5
This printing manufactured exclusively for Books are Fun.

Illustrations by Marianne Richmond

additional illustrations by
Cole Richmond, age 5 and Adam Richmond, age 4

Book design by Sara Dare Biscan

Printed in China

Third Printing

The GIFTs of being Grand

for grandparents everywhere

by Marianne Richmond

Seems like only yesterday,
    your kids were little tykes,
climbing trees, scraping knees,
    and riding bright red bikes.

"*How* did all this time go by?"
    you fondly reminisce
about demanding days long gone
    and pleasures that you miss.

"*G'Bye,* mom and dad," your children now grown
said as they started living life on their own.

In time, there were houses and spouses and pets, new cars and new jobs, some savings and debts.

Hi Mom ... Things are good .... Ya, I could sure use some money ...

"When's Spring Break?"

Dear Mo

I won
hom
the

Job Reviews

The Real World

Deadlines

Adventure...

Ticket

Ticket

Ticket

SOLD

Travel Journal

You wondered, sometimes, as moms and dads do if their plans would include a couple of kids, too.

Just Married

Congrats!

Best Wishes!

TRUE LOVE

Savings Acct.

Rent Bill

Electric Bill

"Kids change your life..."

(But you wouldn't dare pry, 'cause it's just not your place to ask such questions that invade their space.)

Then comes the news, (of course it's unplanned!)

your child is saying you'll soon be a Grand!

"Congratulations!" you say.

"Am I ready?" you muse.

"You're excited?" they ask.

"OF COURSE!" you enthuse.

And while your joy may truly be true,
this grandparenthood thing just happens to you.

No classes or counseling or special instruction
for this once-in-a-lifetime grand induction.

"*A* Grand?" you confirm,
    and to your utter delight,
it feels quite comfy,
    so wonderfully right.

You're instantly smitten
   with cute clothes and shoes
and everything precious
   in pinks and in blues.

Baby Department

"*Welcome,*" you whisper
and know more than maybe
you're head over heels
in love with this baby.

This wee wondrous person
whom you've not met before
starts filling your life
with grand gifts galore.

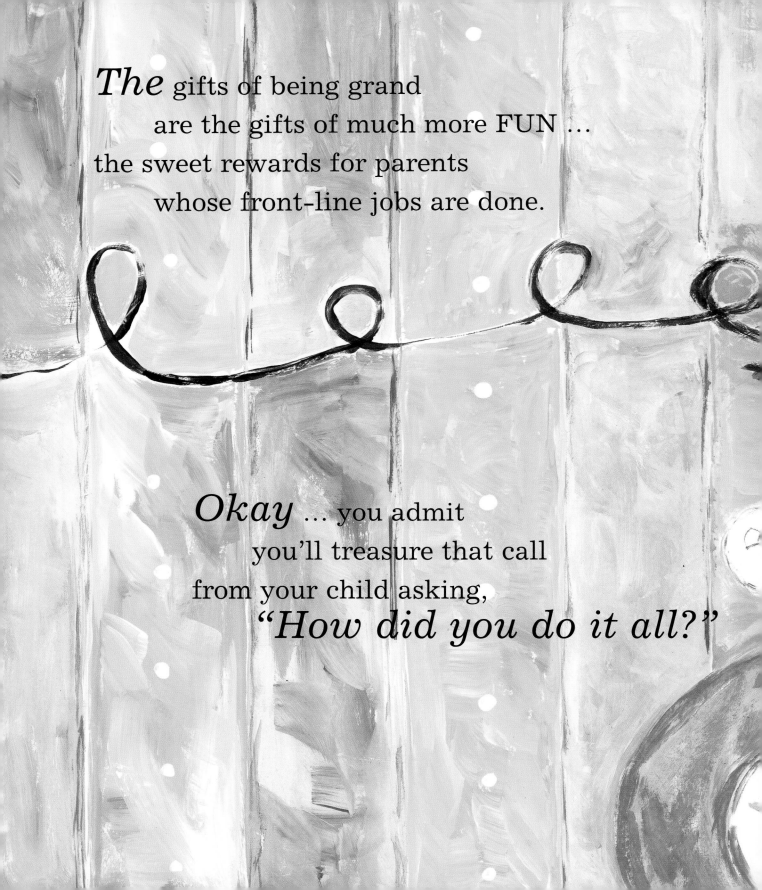

The gifts of being grand
are the gifts of much more FUN ...
the sweet rewards for parents
whose front-line jobs are done.

Okay ... you admit
you'll treasure that call
from your child asking,
"How did you do it all?"

You get permission to spoil
your grandchildren plus
a reason for silliness
and the privilege to fuss.

Your house is for loving
and cuddling and baking,
stories and coloring
and sweet memory making.

You're a popular host
for "you and me" playing
like field trips and shopping
and overnight staying.

And, oh, if you could
you'd buy up that store
to shower your darlings
with cool toys and more!

All this indulging
you'll happily do,
but the greatest of gifts
is what they give you.

A new name for start, an endearing ID,
like Nana or Papa or Grammy or Gee.

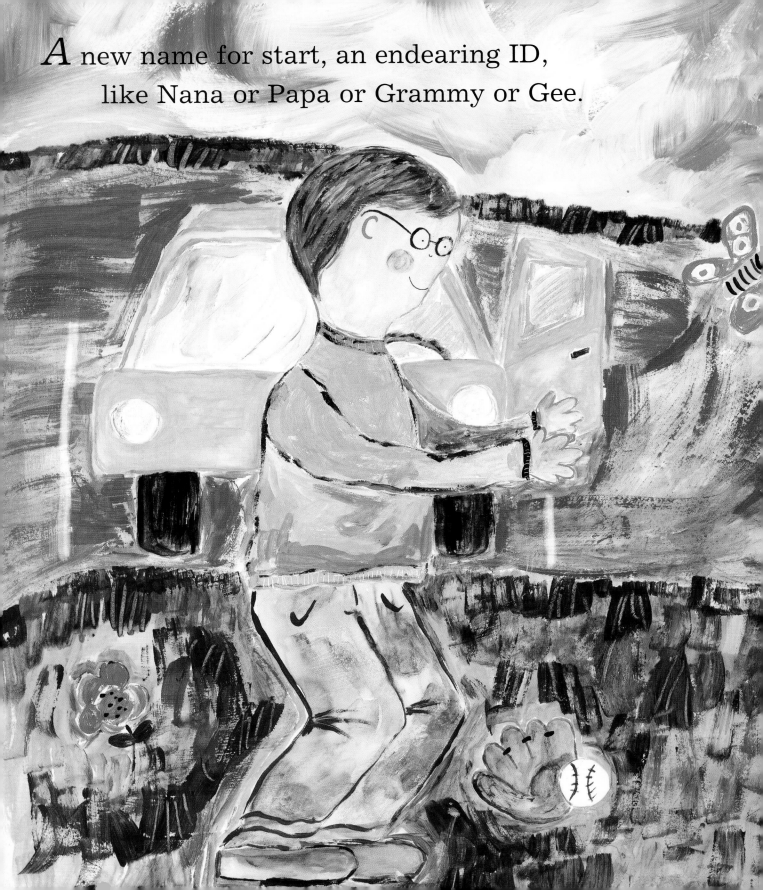

You'll try that name on, though it won't really matter
when it's said by the one whose feet pitter-patter.

Papa!

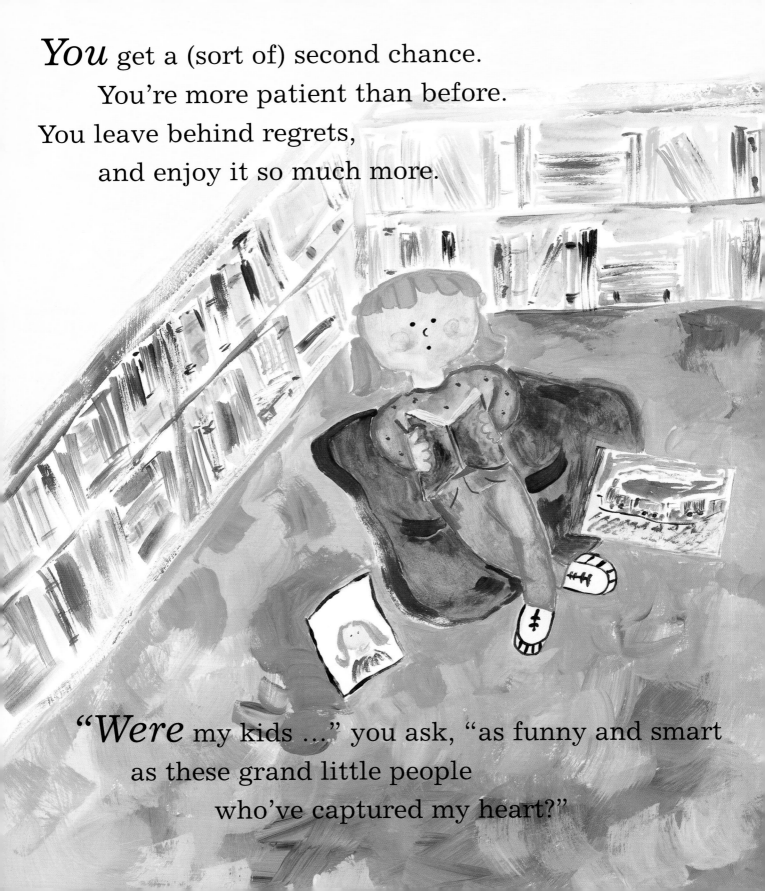

You get a (sort of) second chance.
   You're more patient than before.
You leave behind regrets,
   and enjoy it so much more.

"Were my kids ..." you ask, "as funny and smart
   as these grand little people
      who've captured my heart?"

They beg you to journey
through life at their pace,
discovering adventure
in the simplest place.

Grandchildren give you gladly
a heartfelt invitation
to join them in their world
of play and fascination.

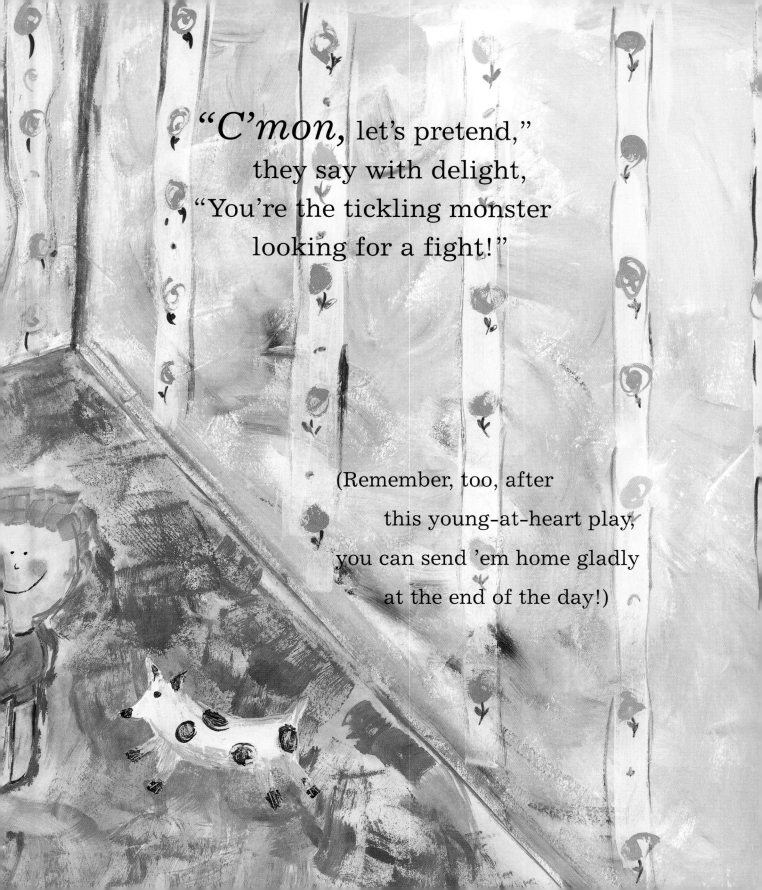

"*C'mon,* let's pretend,"
they say with delight,
"You're the tickling monster
looking for a fight!"

(Remember, too, after
this young-at-heart play,
you can send 'em home gladly
at the end of the day!)

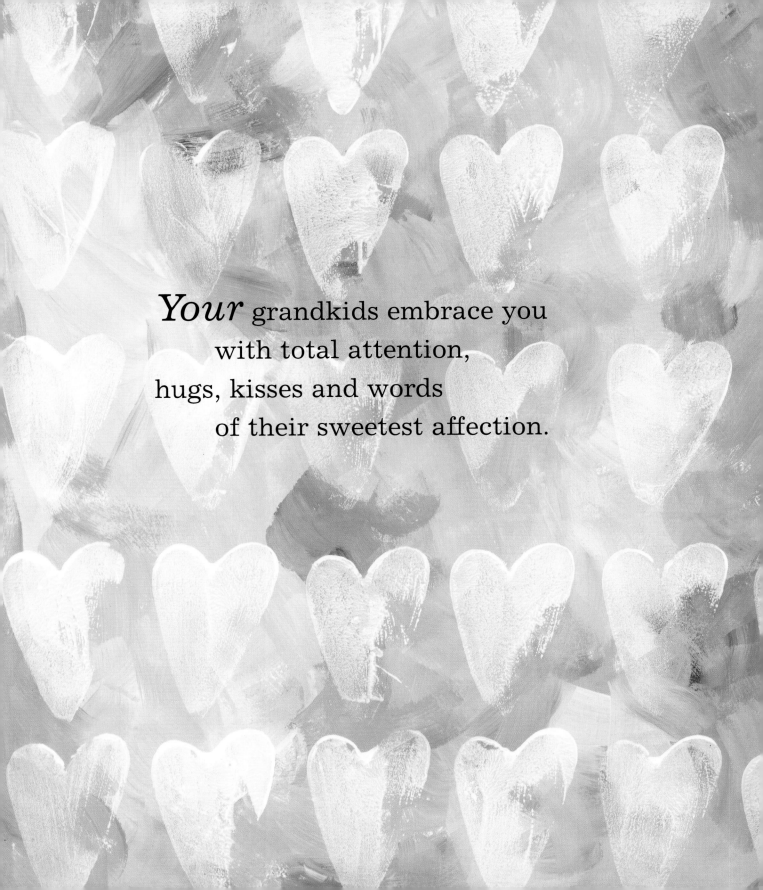

Your grandkids embrace you
with total attention,
hugs, kisses and words
of their sweetest affection.

They'll listen to stories
    of life way back when
their parents were kids
    and what happened then.

To you it seems like yesterday,
    the stories that you tell,
but these kids of your kids
    may have kids someday as well!

For now, just delight in this grand new stage
   that comes when it does, no matter your age.

The best thing of all is the adventure unplanned
   when life gives to you
         the gifts of being grand!

Dear Grandma,
I love you becouse you give me
things and treat me good. You are
the best.

Loves,
Austin
age 8

Dear Grandad,

I love you because you taught
me how to go fishing and use tools.
Thank you for teaching me how!

Your Granddaughter,
Vicki
age: 9

Dear, gramom

I Love you because you are gratiut and best gramom
I ever had. xoxoxoxoxoxo when ever I come over you are
allways their for me. When I need you!!! I don4
o what I would out you!!!!!! do yrht

I Love You gramom

I Love Kevin

Dear Grandpa,
I love you because you are swee
honest, courtious, respectful, and yo
me and my family. Hope it's sunny in
♡ I miss you!
Love, ♡
Rachel
Age 8½

P.S. I can't wait to see you!

Dear Grandmom Ryan,
I love you because
you taught me how to
make gigerbread men.
Love,
Shann
age